Single, Dating, Courting and Informed

(Empowering Tools Before you say "I Do")

Selasi Hodanu-Klu

Copyright © 2018 Selasi Hodanu-Klu All rights reserved.

Single, Dating, Courting and Informed (Empowering Tools Before you say "I Do")

No part of this publication may be reproduced, stored in a retrieval system, or transmitted in any form or by any means, for example, scanned, electronic, recorded, photocopied or published without the prior permission from the author except in the case of brief quotations or non-commercial use accepted by copyright laws.

Scripture quotations marked (NIV) are taken from the Holy Bible, New International Version®, NIV®. Copyright © 1973, 1978, 1984, 2011 by Biblica, Inc.™ Used by permission of Zondervan. All rights reserved worldwide.

The views expressed herein are those of the author and information in this book is intended for informational purpose only. This book provides useful information and hereby is not responsible for any damages, injury or harm.

The reader is responsible for his or her own actions.

Any similarity in terms of an example to real persons, living or dead is coincidental and not intended by the author.

Names and identifying details have been changed to protect the privacy of individuals.

Library of Congress Control Number: 2018910731

Email: selasbooks@gmail.com

ISBN-13: 9781720082095

We invest time into researching on things we want to buy. So must we invest more time in researching and getting to know our prospective partners for a long-lasting and peaceful marriage.

God's timing is always the best and he makes all things beautiful in his time. Wait for his timing.

DEDICATION

This book is dedicated to all my single friends and family who are waiting on God for a happy and fulfilling marriage. May God grant your heart desires swiftly and bless you with a happy, fulfilling and a successful marriage.

Amen.

CONTENTS

1. Single, Dating or Courting..................................15
2. Character..22
3. Know Each Other's Background..............................31
4. Don't Ignore Red Flags....................................38
5. Build Self-Esteem and Know Your Worth.....................47
6. Work on Your Past and Don't Drag it Along.................58
7. Avoid Pretence and Be Yourself............................64
8. Practice Abstinence.......................................69
9. Sexual Abstinence Doesn't Equate to Ignorance.............79
10. Don't Jump Into Marriage.................................84
11. Don't Be Desperate.......................................90
12. Build Friendship...95
13. Set Boundaries..100
14. Why Do I Date The Wrong People?.........................107
15. Prepare to be a Godly Wife or Husband...................113
16. Will I be Sexually Compatible?..........................125
17. Communication is a Vital Tool...........................127
18. Do You Think You're Ready to Say "I do"?................131
19. The Wedding is Less Than 10 hours, Plan it Wisely...137
20. During and After The Honeymoon..........................141

Questions to Ponder On......................................145
Notes...147
Final Thought...149
Acknowledgments...151
About the Author..152

Introduction

Misconceptions about singlehood, dating, and courtship have become stumbling blocks for successful marriages. Being single does not make you a failure or a weakling. This period is for learning, self-development, and self-recognition. This time period helps to identify what is acceptable to you in a relationship and therefore marriage. The experience from pre-marital relationships can be used as building blocks to build a fun, peaceful, and successful marriage. Failed pre-marital relationships should not be considered as loses but rather learning experiences.

The ability to love yourself, for example, is very essential for a successful relationship because the way you love yourself sets a standard for you to be loved and to reciprocate love. If you are not whole as a single man or woman, you cannot easily accept the marriage union and its responsibilities.

Marriage is not the key to happiness in life and not being loved by someone or not being in a relationship doesn't define who you are. You are who God made you to be, your presence in this world really counts regardless of your marital status and you can make an impact whether single or married.

This book will empower you to be able to develop a sound and healthy relationship. There are a lot of red flags that can be seen while in a relationship but tend to be ignored or excuses made for them. Reality tends to set in sooner or later and so are consequential regrets, therefore, "Watch and Pray".

This book will also help you in choosing a person with the qualities you truly want and it will guide your motives and expectations in marriage. It will empower you adequately with some relevant tools to guide you before finally saying "I do".

Enjoy!!!!!!!

CHAPTER 1

Single, Dating or Courting

Single: In my opinion, a person who is single is someone who is not in any kind of relationship and has a goal of meeting someone for a committed relationship. It involves spending time with the prospective gentleman or lady to get to know their personality. Getting to know this prospective person should be in both group settings, such as in the company of friends and families for you to know how they treat them and also in one-on-one settings. The qualities that are seen are matched with the desired realistic qualities that a single person will like in their prospective partner. Sometimes, some of those preferred qualities are compromised on as a single person ages or becomes more experienced and matured which may come with its ups and downs.

The list of qualities usually depends on age, maturity, and background. For example, a 20 year old may have a very long list of qualities and will want to see all those qualities in a person. They may even deem a person who has 80% of those qualities as unfit. A 30-year-old for example due to their experiences may compromise for 80% or less of the qualities they want. This is because they have become more matured and realized that certain qualities are not assured keys to a committed and prosperous relationship.

As these desirable qualities are being sought from a prospective partner, so should a single person endeavor to possess desirable qualities for their prospective partner. There is no perfect person in this world and sometimes, the prospective partner will need your help to develop some good qualities you desire in them.

The person you meet may be an "unpolished gem", but your patience, wisdom, encouragement, and love will make them a "Crown Jewel" to behold.

Certain people's packages may come with 80% of the good qualities you desire and may need some work on their 20%. Will you give the opportunity to find out what that 20% is? Are you willing to help to accomplish the 20%? You may have regrets after you find out that someone worked on that 20% for them to become the "Crown Jewel" you desired.

Dating: Involves no actual commitment and may have a short lifespan. The dating process is where a lady and a gentleman begin to know each other. It is the process of finding a suitable partner who you may deem right and qualified to become your spouse. Dating begins with some form of physical attraction and interest in a person. One can therefore not pinpoint the existence of true love at this stage because it may end up being infatuation.

One needs to "find" themselves first and feel complete before entering into this venture. There's no assurance that the person you may date will complete you or be the missing piece to your life puzzle. They may rather need you to complete them by becoming the missing piece in their puzzle.

This process usually involves lots of socialization. There is the tendency of being petty over little things such as the way he/she dresses, too much makeup or chewing with the mouth open etc. Such things are taken into consideration when making the decision to take the relationship to another level.

This process is like an interviewer screening a potential employee to determine if they fit into the organization's culture and goals. If they do not fit the culture and goals or they think they cannot train the person to become a good fit, they may choose to move on. When a person does not fit into the profile, there is no need to try to fit them into it, especially when they are not ready to be fitted or to work at it. Sometimes, certain changes and sacrifices can be made for the person to become a right fit but that person must be willing to change if not, it would breed frustration and a waste of time.

Most people make or have made lots of mistakes

in judging too quickly. This has resulted in the loss of very good marriage materials or marriageable people while others have married people they regret getting married to.

I have talked to people who have regretted marrying or not marrying someone they dated and judged as being either perfect or imperfect for them. The dating period is the time to pause, pray, watch and ask God to direct you in choosing the right partner. During the dating process, a person can decide to quickly move on with another date because there are no deep commitments.

It is very common to see people compromising their Godly standards, principles, lifestyles and good morals to secure a date. Do not compromise your moral standards for any reason in order to secure and maintain a date. It is common at this stage for people to portray themselves as who they are not in order for the other party to find them as a perfect fit. A person at this point can be attracted to one's physique, spirituality, intelligence, etc. but as the process moves on, one may discover there is more to a relationship than that particular thing they were attracted to initially. This process may sometimes seem complicated, but watching and praying, and seeking direction from God makes it smoother and enables one to make a good decision.

Note: Behaviors that are accepted and visible during dating are transferred to the courtship stage and then into marriage, therefore, WATCH and PRAY.

Courting: This is the stage that the relationship becomes exclusive and the decision to take it a step further (marriage) is made. Courtship is basically about nurturing the plant of love that germinated during the dating process into maturity.

This is where commitment kicks in and matters of the heart are discussed. Deep friendship is built at this stage, couples get to know each other more, and are introduced to families and friends. Conversations at this stage of the relationship entail future plans of the family such as the number of children, where to live, etc. Couples may also talk about the kind of wedding ceremony they want, expectations in marriage, ways of raising children and getting to know each other's entire background.

It is important for both parties to be open to

each other during this period. This is because information disclosed at this stage gives the insight for parties to decide on saying "I Do", to part peacefully or go their separate ways. The courtship environment is one that allows love to grow freely and the foundation of trust to be built. During this period, behaviors that are considered to be one's weakness are discussed and solutions sought for.

Make adequate time to watch and pray during this period because decisions made at this time will either make or mar your marriage and future.

CHAPTER 2

Character

Matthew 12:35 (NIV)
A good man brings good things out of the good stored up in him, and an evil man brings evil things out of the evil stored up in him.

Character is very important in life's race and it defines you. It will also make or mar you therefore, character can ensure your success or be a snare to it. It is said, "a bad character is like a car with a flat tire, and it takes you nowhere".

A person's character is developed by nature and

nurture (life's experiences). One can decide to use those experiences to develop a good character or a bad one. How do you truly define your personality and character? How do you act with or without pressure? A bad character cannot be hidden. Just like pregnancy, it will eventually be seen.

Galatians 5:22-23 (NIV)

22 But the fruit of the Spirit is love, joy, peace, forbearance, kindness, goodness, faithfulness, 23 gentleness and self-control. Against such things there is no law.

The bible talks about the fruit of the spirit in the above scripture where Christian character is basically defined with such characteristics. The character of self-control is fundamental to all the fruits of the spirit mentioned in the above scripture. The way and manner in which you control yourself by deeds and words are very important and a test of character.

Self-control is one major practice in life when exercised in all spheres of life will take you places and will avoid drama in your life. If you're single and looking for a spouse, character is one important attribute that a man or woman looks out for in order to decide on dating, courtship or marriage. Your character may or may not attract a potential husband or wife and may be a great opportunity lost due to the first impression, therefore, always develop and put up a good character.

Sometimes, people don't make time to try to know you before they judge your character. They watch the way you relate to your friends, family, loved ones, subordinates, superiors or anybody around you. They also observe your words, gesture, and poise to define or judge your character. They also watch the way you treat children, the disabled, the poor, the rich, and the elderly to easily define the kind of person you truly are.

1 Corinthians 15:33 (NIV)
Do not be misled: "Bad company corrupts good character."

Some people believe in this verse to the fault, so they wouldn't give chances to be around a person with a bad character. No matter how attractive you are or your status in society, they would not want to associate with you or give you the opportunity to prove yourself worthy of their time, attention or love. This is because your bad character blinds them to the good qualities you possess.

Sometimes, missing the opportunity to impress someone the very first time may cost you because you lose the ability to prove yourself again.

Titus 2:7-8 (NIV)
7 In everything set them an example by doing what is good. In your teaching show integrity, seriousness 8 and soundness of speech that cannot be condemned, so that those who oppose you may be ashamed because they have nothing bad to say about us.

It is said that, integrity is an expensive attribute that doesn't come cheap, neither can it be expected from cheap people. It involves consistency rather than a one-off thing. If you don't have or develop integrity, it cannot come easily to you. It is an attribute that must therefore be worked on.

If integrity is an embedded principle, it fosters a genuine relationship because trust in a relationship is a product of integrity. When you walk in integrity, you call a spade a spade rather than a big spoon because of circumstances. This attitude makes marriages thrive because spouses are rest assured that the truth will always come from their partner. If integrity is a key in your life, it transcends into being faithful and honest with one's partner.

Mark 10:45 (NIV)

For even the Son of Man did not come to be served, but to serve, and to give his life as a ransom for many."

Humility is also another great virtue. Is it your badge of honor, or pride and arrogance take the most part of you? Humility is a great virtue since the bible said the son of man came to serve and not to be served.

Serving people in any form or means is great, very important and pleasing to God. Even though one cannot give his life as Christ did for us, serving one another is a great attribute which sustains a healthy relationship and marriage.

If you don't learn how to serve people around you, you cannot wholeheartedly and easily serve your spouse. You will find it as a difficult task to do and will eventually get worked out doing it. Service is less burdensome if it is done wholeheartedly with no strings attached.

Character

James 1:19-20 (NIV)
19 My dear brothers and sisters, take note of this: Everyone should be quick to listen, slow to speak and slow to become angry, 20 because human anger does not produce the righteousness that God desires.

Are you quick to listen and slow to speak or you are the argumentative type where everything or topic becomes a point of argument for you? I have come across ladies who present themselves very well but whatever comes from their mouth is like venom, very nauseating and distasteful. They pride themselves in being rude, saucy, repulsive, awful and quick to speak their minds. The results that one will derive from such a distasteful character are messy relationships, trouble, and repulsion of people. Sometimes, it is not easy to hold your peace but assessing one's self and words would be very appropriate and so is choosing when to use words.

The scripture also talks about anger which ruins relationships, makes people bitter, unforgiving and is poisonous to one's health. Some people know they have problems controlling their anger hence they use it as an excuse for their unpleasant behaviors. The least misunderstanding becomes a big ruckus which can escalate into physical aggression. It's because of uncontrollable anger that some spouses beat up their partners.

Luke 6:31(NIV)

Do to others as you would have them do to you. A conscious effort to treat people the way you want to be treated would make the world a better place. Usually, we dish out behaviors and attitudes to our fellow human beings without thinking about the effect or putting ourselves in their shoes. We just do it and expect relationships to thrive by such actions and behaviors. Careful considerations of how we treat people and being sensitive to others feelings demonstrate a good character.

How do you treat your fellow human beings? The way you treat other people correlates with the way you treat your partner in a relationship. If you're used to having no empathy, you will do the same in your relationship.

It is also a plausible idea to look beyond material things and concentrate on character in a relationship leading to marriage. More often than not, you hear ladies talk about the desire to date no other person than a rich man and they relegate good character to the background or to the bottom of their list of desires. They focus on the wealth and don't care whether they're being maltreated or disrespected. Such relationships are sometimes not enjoyed but rather endured because of constant abuse that may eventually lead to the loss of life. For some, the focus is not wealth but, educational, religious or social status.

My advice to those who have this mentality is to consider what their fate would be when the material things fade away. Beauty fades and material things can also be lost, but character stands the test of time. Material things and one's status must not be the main determinants of choosing a partner. If the person comes with these material things, that's a plus for you but if they don't and possess very great qualities and character, it surpasses all things.

This is because, with character, time and chance can make these material things come your way. Over a period of time, you will eventually realize that, money, status, fame, and material things do not assure happiness and therefore sacrificing your happiness for them will eventually wear you down. Character, (Humility, Integrity, Service, etc.) are the keys to enjoying a happy and lasting relationship.

As much as you can never get to know 100% of a person's character before or after marriage, it's always a good idea to give the relationship a little more time in order to get to know the person. Good character stands the test of time and so will a bad character eventually be exposed because it cannot be hidden hence give it time for it to prove itself.

Philippians 4:8 (NIV)

Finally, brothers and sisters, whatever is true, whatever is noble, whatever is right, whatever is pure, whatever is lovely, whatever is admirable—if anything is excellent or praiseworthy—think about such things.

CHAPTER 3

Know Each Other's Background

When a person is single, dating or courting, it is very easy to ignore the need to know their partner's background in making a decision about marriage. People are usually blinded by love and the zeal for marriage, thereby forgetting to know each other's background. Seeking information into a person's past and also information regarding their health, educational background, etc. is very crucial before marriage.

Know Each Other's Background

Information pertaining to their past, such as mistakes, adventures, failures etc. must be divulged. Family health history such as genetic diseases, genotype, etc. must also be enquired for decisions to be made appropriately. If this information is known, it becomes easier for the couple to make a decision on marriage. It enables them to decide whether to deal with the issues as and when they arise, work on a solution together or to end the relationship.

When there is fore-knowledge, couples are better prepared to deal with issues rather than having "surprises" pop up in the marriage. For instance, if you're of African, South and Central American descent, it is important to know your genotype and that of the person you intend to marry. This is because of a disease known as Sickle Cell Anemia which causes the red blood cells in a person's body to be shaped like a sickle instead of a disk. This results in severe pain in the joints, organ failure, strokes, etc., and eventually death.

Knowing a person's financial responsibilities, debts, spending and saving habits etc. are also important. This is because, by implication, couple's

Know Each Other's Background

become part of their spouse's financial dealings. Parties must inform each other of their student's loans, credit card debts, and other debts incurred prior to meeting them because, trying to pay off unending debts can have a significant toll on the relationship.

Financial issues are a major cause of fights, arguments, and divorce, therefore, it must be given a high priority in the marriage decision making. When seeking or sharing such information, it may seem as though you're seeking or sharing too much information but as said earlier, this knowledge will help you to be better prepared.

The belief of a person also has an immense effect on the relationship. Questions such as the style of raising children, sharing of all information with your spouse, be it health, financial and passwords must be asked. What is their belief when it comes to the body being the temple of God and therefore what goes in affects the temple such as drug abuse, smoking, alcohol intake, etc.? You may view it as trivial to consider these things because you're in love but it can eventually put a wedge in the marriage.

Know Each Other's Background

Do not assume that you do not need to seek the background of a prospective partner that you meet in a familiar territory or is known to other people. This is because you will face the consequences when you do not do your due diligence of getting to know their background and who they truly are. Don't rely on people's judgment about a person and jump into marriage with them, do your personal investigations.

You will never know if you don't ask questions as my mom always said. She believed that, if you don't ask certain questions before entering into a marriage union, you may not have the opportunity to ask again because it will be considered as being petty or nagging. According to her, if you don't ask prior to marriage, your partner would assume you don't mind not knowing about them and you can deal with such issues in marriage when they come up.

Hosea 4:6a (NIV)

My people are destroyed from lack of knowledge.
The bible talks about people perishing due to lack of knowledge. If you're not in the know of information that could be vital to your life, you could perish literarily.

Know Each Other's Background

Communication and information are very vital before and during the marriage and this cannot be overemphasized. Ask any information that crosses your mind, dissect it, analyze it and make sure you're comfortable and at peace with the answer.

Questions such as, do you have any child or children that you are aware or may not be aware of? Should I expect any drama from your family or friends? What is your financial status? Do you believe in celibacy? Do you believe in a monogamous relationship? How do you react when you're angry? Is it okay for me to have access to your phone anytime? Do you have any aliases? Are there any genetic diseases in your family?

Do you have any addictions or fantasies? What is your perspective on giving? Do you believe in tithing? What do you do if all hope seems lost? Do you resort to God or you throw tantrums? Do you believe in helping your wife around the house? Answers to such questions prepare you to deal with problems that may come when you get married.

Ephesians 4:18 (NIV)
They are darkened in their understanding and

separated from the life of God because of the ignorance that is in them due to the hardening of their hearts.

Ignorance is bliss and no excuse can be given to defy the consequences that come with ignorance, therefore if anything bothers your mind, ask. Do not feel you're asking too many questions because the time to ask is before you commit yourself into a lasting relationship. For some people, it is difficult for them to volunteer any information without you asking. They feel they are giving out too much information without you asking. Use the dating and courting period to seek information that you deem necessary to equip yourself appropriately.

Some people also agree to keep their relationship discreet from friends and loved ones which may be dangerous. As the relationship develops into a very serious one, trusted friends and family must be aware of it and going for activities and programs together are very important.

As the saying goes, "Nobody is an island", a friend or family may know your partner's secret lifestyle, background or secret spouse which you

Know Each Other's Background

may never get to know. If you're seen together, people also watch out for you by seeking information regarding each other's background and lifestyle.

As much as some of your family and friends information may be bias, lies or exaggerations, you have the knowledge and ability to investigate and if possible talk about it. You can never be wrong in taking time to know and investigate each other's background since it will help you in making one of the most important decisions called marriage.

CHAPTER 4

Don't Ignore Red Flags

Don't ignore or overlook the signs of trouble in a relationship. When driving, we stop at the sight of danger. Just as we stop when we see signs of danger, so should we stop and investigate when we see signs of danger in a relationship. For instance, a man or woman who insults you or is rude to you in a relationship will continue in marriage. If a person disrespects you, your siblings, and parents, they will eventually disrespect you. The habit of throwing tantrums, punching and kicking walls when angry, will eventually result in physical abuse. Instead of making excuses for such actions, analyze them and make a good decision. A cheating partner before marriage will likely be an adulterer after marriage. Don't ignore certain signs or brush them under the carpet because if the carpet becomes choked with dirt, it spills over without notice.

Song of Songs 2:15 (NIV)
Catch for us the foxes, the little foxes that ruin the vineyards, our vineyards that are in bloom.

The little foxes of life are the little things that are overlooked especially at the beginning of a relationship. They grow like thorns to choke the beauty and the future of a happy marriage.

Some danger signs are very obvious and cannot be ignored in a relationship. The problem is, some couples either decide not to notice them or one party thinks it will cease over a period of time.

There are some people who may be so much in love to notice the signs and see friends and family who point them out as enemies. Excuses and lies may last for the season of fresh love, but with time, they become too obvious and too late to fix, which gives way for divorce to creep in.

The safest thing to do once you notice such danger signs which indicate potential threats to your marriage is to either walk away or find a mutual solution to fix them. Pay attention to details in your relationship because the little foxes may rear their heads in the form of verbal abuse, physical abuse, emotional abuse, manipulation, argumentative lifestyles, autocracy or control, cheating, lies, anger, and laziness.

Verbal abuse is where the person uses words such as, "you're nobody, you're a weakling, you're not smart, you're so dumb, you're not good enough, you're lucky being with me, you're ugly, you're not pretty," etc. Such a person will destroy your self-worth and esteem making you see yourself as the words you're being described with.

Physical abuse is where you are hit with objects, fist or foot. Love is not supposed to hurt but to be enjoyed. If you are in a relationship where you're being physically hit, seek help because it will get worse when you get married and this may eventually lead to an untimely or premature death. Do not make excuses for the abuser or cover-up with lies because you're made to feel it was your fault they hit you. The abuser may ask for forgiveness and promise not to repeat it but more often than not, it happens again or will happen again. This behavior eventually becomes an unending cycle until one day, an accident happens where the victim loses their life.

Emotional abuse involves a person ignoring you, refusing to acknowledge your feelings, always doing things intentionally to hurt you or for you to keep complaining. He or she may go for days without contacting you, won't respond to your call or text and when they do, they show no remorse and use words like, "you're too sensitive" etc.

They try to invalidate your emotions by not empathizing with you nor calm you down when the situation demands it. They may even ridicule your feelings and opinions in the bid to make you do things their way. Love is not selfish and abusive but rather gentle and selfless.

Manipulation is when the person preys on your compassion and love to make you do things that you will usually not do. They use their experience and skill to manipulate you. Such a person will make you feel like you're irrational or insensitive the day you decide not to succumb to their manipulation.

An Argumentative person is also someone who is always willing to start an argument just to win it. Arguments are like a game to them and they cannot go a day without it. Every topic of discussion turns into an argument where they become very defensive and critical of you even when it does not pertain to the topic. Such a person thinks that they're always right so they hardly accept their faults. Even if you go the extra mile for them, they don't appreciate it, neither does it mean anything to them.

In an autocratic relationship, one party controls every aspect of the relationship. This may include deciding on what their partner should wear, even the kind of words they have to use during a normal conversation, etc. The partner who controls the relationship becomes abusive sooner or later. They also attack the judgment of their partners which eventually leads to timidity and loss of self-esteem.

Another red flag is cheating. Some people who cheat in marriage or commit adultery had the tendency or cheated prior to marriage. It is ok to forgive and give second chances when the offender takes steps to work on their flaws. This does not mean that you should condone to serial occurrences. For instance, there would be no need to keep a man or woman who is constantly flirting with others, cheats and come back to tell you unending stories. Some may even be emboldened by your leniency to the extent of making inappropriate overtures to other women or men in your presence.

Cheating is a personal decision and someone who values a relationship will not cheat on their partner. The decision to cheat reflects the value bestowed on the relationship.

A person who lies about everything, for instance, cannot be trusted. Little lies become humongous ones whereby one cannot even be trusted when they are genuinely speaking the truth. Some people claim they lie because they don't want their loved ones to be hurt. They become habitual liars with no iota of truth in their being. Lying eventually breaks down a marriage because marriage cannot thrive on lies. Flee when you notice a person is a habitual liar because when you get married, heartache will be your daily bread. Such habitual liars are very uncomfortable when speaking the truth because of the habit of lying and therefore must seek divine help from God and counseling.

Another red flag is anger. Anger can also be very bad even though it may not result in physical or verbal abuse. Such people don't usually take jokes and fume over issues that everybody is laughing at. They hold on to issues for days without letting go, would not discuss them nor accept an apology. They are usually not fun to be with and you mostly have to watch your words when speaking to or dealing with them. They may also be jealous, and wouldn't want to see you talking to another man or woman though they can be very loving and caring which is usually confusing. With such a person, you will always be in the mode of singing daily apologies.

The Couch potatoes are also the kind of people who target hardworking men or women for a relationship. They use their words and love to coax their women or men into staying with them. They prey on them, know exactly what they want to hear, how they want to be treated and they work hard to deliver such actions promptly. Such people will give every little excuse not to find a job or even keep a job and will end up on the couch week after week while their partner runs around to bring the bacon home. They are professionals in this trade of using others to get what they want.

Proverbs 10:4-5 (NIV)

4 Lazy hands make for poverty, but diligent hands bring wealth. 5 He who gathers crops in summer is a prudent son, but he who sleeps during harvest is a disgraceful son.

According to the verse above, "lazy hands make poverty, but intelligent hands bring wealth", work is needed to be financially sustainable, therefore, do not entertain someone who won't put in any effort into becoming financially sustainable.

Red flags are gradually seen in a relationship but it must not be assumed that they will go away on their own as they appear. Unfortunately, such red flags peak after a lot of time and love have been invested in the relationship for one to quit easily.

Being caught up in such a precarious situation,

there's a tendency of not being able to confide in family or friends and just go along to accept the red flag because of familiarity. Such little foxes must intentionally, consciously and strategically tackled, because if they're not fixed, they get worse in marriage.

Finally, try to evaluate and correct these signs as much as possible with prayer and lifestyle changes or behavior patterns. Please encourage the person to seek professional help and seek God when such behaviors are exhibited and don't downplay them by making excuses for them. A person who loves you would be willing to work on themselves to change their behavior in order to make you happy. If you realize you cannot deal with it, don't commit yourself into marriage, because such behaviors magnify themselves in marriage as compared to the microscopic view during the dating and courtship period. No reason should be good enough during a pre-marital relationship for you to enter into a bad marriage. Stop the little foxes before it's too late to destroy your dream of a happy marriage.

CHAPTER 5

Build Self-Esteem and Know Your Worth

Jeremiah 1:5 (NIV)
"Before I formed you in the womb I knew you,
before you were born I set you apart;
I appointed you as a prophet to the nations".

Before God formed you in your mother's womb, he knew you were going to exist according to the book of Jeremiah, that's why among all the sperms that traveled on the journey, you came out victoriously. You didn't lose the battle on the way to the egg but made it sound and safely and was declared the winner of the game. This for a fact proves that God has a purpose for you no matter what you may have gone through in life, he hasn't finished with you yet.

He set you apart from all others hence your uniqueness. This uniqueness must be the stepping stone to acceptance of your worth and building your self-esteem. You were set apart means, you were purposely created. Therefore, there is no one like you. You are a unique and special individual no matter how people describe your face, your shape, intelligence, achievements, etc. Once you have life, shake the negativities off, tell yourself you're better than those negativities, and you will be a better person. Jeremiah 1:5 states how God has appointed you a prophet to the nations.

If God chose to appoint you as a prophet to the nations, he has literally sent you into this world to make an impact wherever your feet steps on to. He just wants you to brighten the corner where you are and let your little light shine wherever you find yourself. Your self-esteem and how you perceive yourself is very important to him because you're the carrier of the change he wants in the world by the impact you make.

Psalm 139:13-14 (NIV)
¹³For you created my inmost being;
you knit me together in my mother's womb.
¹⁴I praise you because I am fearfully and wonderfully made; your works are wonderful,
I know that full well.

You were fearfully and wonderfully made by God to impact the world no matter your physique, situation, background, status or your past. His handiwork is always beautiful no matter how people perceive you and he knitted you perfectly together in your mother's womb which makes you a unique individual and a complete person in his sight.

Tilly didn't build her self-esteem before she got married. She was always verbally abused by her husband who she got to know a few months before they got married. His words always broke her and she felt less of a woman. After their divorce, she still didn't pick up her self-esteem and self-worth and entered into another relationship which ended within a year of marriage. She realized she had to work on her self-esteem and worth.

If you don't build self-esteem, you will feel insecure and will fall prey to anyone who comes around and shows a little security. Your insecurity can be vividly seen so you will be beaten to the game with the pretence of offering your needs. The fact that you don't know your self-worth, you will think that's the best treatment and will not want to lose it even if you're disrespected and maltreated.

Knowing one's self-worth is the bedrock of a respectful relationship. If you know what you're worth and carry yourself as such, you look out to attract people who are like you or are on the same page with you. Knowing your self-worth and cherishing self-respect will not allow you to attract "grown boys or girls". You will attract grown and responsible men who love, cherish and value women and grown women who respect and cherish men in a relationship.

When you don't compromise on your self-respect and esteem, people respect you for taking that stand and value you as an asset they must cherish. Far too many men prey on women who don't value their self-worth and treat them anyhow because they know they can get away with such a behavior and so do some women also treat men who don't build their self-esteem. Don't settle for abuse whether physical or emotional. Disrespectful and hurtful words are forms of abuse that must not be tolerated by both men and women.

When you value yourself, dating such a person will not exist in your world. It's even worse when it's tolerated in marriage. This is because it becomes a daily occurrence even in the presence of children. The children grow up seeing this as normal because children look up to parents and tend to grow up disrespecting the institution of marriage.

Growing up in my teenage years, my dad used to tell us that he doesn't believe in divorce but he would never allow any man to lay a finger on his daughters. This made me really value myself so much, because I knew he valued us and would not want any man to treat us as a punching bag. I therefore had that at the back of my mind while searching for love because I was armed with that information.

The price tag you place on yourself is the price you will be bought. Nobody goes to the shop and asks for an increase in the price of an item before purchase. They either bargain for a price reduction or buy the item at the listed price. Before a politician comes into power, they campaign, make promises and win our votes. After they are in power, they stop campaigning and the same way a man will woo you into his bed with nice words, gifts, etc. and after you give in, he sees it as normal and won't respect that "honorable gold-mine".

Inferiority complex in some people is a big challenge they face inwardly every day. For some people, the words used to describe them during childhood or when growing up affects their self-esteem so badly they can hardly pick their pieces and recoup to become who God wants them to become. Rejection and harsh words can break a person but once they don't break your bones, you have another chance at building your self-esteem with the direction of the Holy Spirit and the renewal of your mind.

Build Self-Esteem and Know Your Worth

Psalm 34:18 (NIV)
The LORD is close to the brokenhearted and saves those who are crushed in spirit.

Don't believe you are of little value by comparing yourself with others, because your presence in this world matters no matter your background.

I always encourage parents to speak positively into their children's lives. Dads especially should affirm their daughters with words that would build them up because they end up looking out for such words in men. My dad really contributed to building my self-esteem. He always encouraged me and never allowed me to give up doing any task. He believed in me more than I believed in myself and my mom taught me my self-worth as a woman and how to carry myself as well as see myself as a lady who deserves a man who will treat me well.

My parents by this act built me up and I told myself I deserve nothing but the best in life and would not settle for mediocrity. In looking for a life partner, I applied these things my parents instilled in me and I was very cautious because I didn't want to make a mistake.

When parents start building their children up with "you can do it", "you are a pretty girl", "you are a very handsome boy", "you're very intelligent", etc. children grow up to live those words and look out for people who believe in them.

Jeremiah 31:3 (NIV)

The LORD appeared to us in the past, saying: "I have loved you with an everlasting love; I have drawn you with unfailing kindness.

God loves you regardless of what society may think of you. He can always place you where he deems fit because he really cares about you and you are not insignificant. You are worth his time and that's why Christ died for you. He didn't only die for people high in society, the rich or the well-accomplished. He equally died for the poor, brokenhearted or rejected.

Psalm 69:20 (NIV)

Scorn has broken my heart and has left me helpless; I looked for sympathy, but there was none, for comforters, but I found none.

If you wallow in sympathy and self-pity, you will not get out from the feeling of rejection and of no value. You have to purpose in your heart that enough is enough and you want to start life feeling great about yourself and moving forward in victory.

Proverbs 31:25 (NIV)

She is clothed with strength and dignity;

she can laugh at the days to come.

Most men are attracted to women who know and understand their self-worth and are confident about themselves. A woman must be happy with whom she truly is and with or without a man's compliment, she knows she is beautiful and confident.

If you're clothed with strength and dignity, you seek a man who will protect your dignity and not take you for granted. Your strength attracts great and like-minded people to you. They see what you see in yourself, and have no choice than to admire it. Even if you're down, your strength and self-worth will encourage you to pick up your pieces and start running with the dependence on God as your shield. When people tell me I found myself a good man, I tell them he is rather blessed to have found me because I know I complement him in so many ways.

More often than not, people rather tell women how they found themselves good men but barely tell the men they found themselves good women. If you are able to validate yourself, you don't need to be validated by anybody. If a woman understands her worth, she makes herself valuable and a real man will respect that.

Some ladies believe and hold on to the notion of looking out for or attracting and dating "bad boys".

According to them, they are attracted to such bad boys because it is very thrilling to date them. They believe that the idea of the "bad boys" taking them through a roller-coaster ride in the relationship keeps them on their toes. They always look out for the "bad boys" and such boys end up breaking their heart always.

If you build your self-worth and esteem, you will not look out for "bad boys" because a serious relationship involves two adults who want to achieve a common goal in life which a "bad boy" cannot give you. A matured gentleman can act like the "bad boy" you want when the time comes for him to act as such but won't live a "bad boy" life.

2 Timothy 1:7 (NIV)
For the Spirit God gave us does not make us

timid, but gives us power, love and self-discipline. Timidity is a killer of self-esteem and self-worth. It diminishes your potential, drives your urge to blossom down the drain and makes you unable to fulfill your full potential and ability. Some people become so timid in life they cannot even speak up if they're being maltreated by their partner or spouse because they fear they will leave them or it will make them mad. Most people prey on timid people and repeat behaviors that they dislike because they know they will not vent or speak up.

My dear lady or gentleman, you don't need to be rude but if your partner's behavior is unacceptable to you, don't hesitate in making them aware. If you do not stop certain behaviors in their tracks before they become the norm, you will eventually lose yourself.

In order to appreciate love and enjoy it, you have to love yourself first because it makes it easier for you to accept love and reciprocate it. Let your self-worth and self-esteem carry you through life's challenges and relationships and you will be happy you developed them.

CHAPTER 6

Work on Your Past and Don't Drag it Along

You may have been hurt in the past but this happens in the lives of most people who have ever been in a relationship. The baggage of past relationships may come in the form of depression, disappointments, insecurity, hurt, anger and others. As much as we cannot turn the hands of time to erase those bitter experiences, we have the ultimate power to stop their effect in our lives and to start life afresh. Christ will help mend your broken pieces. The potter wants to put you back together again if you let him and rely on him.

When Christ fixes you, you move forward from your hurt and will not hold on to the bitterness and hate. He will give you a reason to start with a clean slate, a purpose and hope to look into the bright future. The hurt and bitterness from people's past experiences doesn't allow them to give anybody a chance again. All men and women are branded the same and no one is given the slightest chance to work on building a lasting relationship. With the help of God, one can be hopeful in trying a new relationship and such a person must not be blinded to red flags or genuine love. They must be cautious but not overly critical. Taking time to heal, grow and working on one's self for a while is very important.

This is because, if you do not heal from the hurt from the past, but you rather jump into the next promising and available relationship, you will end up being hurt again. Possibly, you will be viewing your current relationship through the lens of the hurt from your past. Insecurity, for example, is such a killer in a relationship. If you have been insecure in your past relationships, it is time to learn to build trust within yourself and for others.

Not all men are the same and so are women. Everybody is unique in their own right and until they prove to be unfaithful or show signs for you to feel insecure. Building trust takes time and seeking answers from your partner helps to allay all the unnecessary suspicions and assumptions. Being insecure may result in acting wrongly and also sometimes overreacting when there is no need for it.

Sometimes, certain behaviors and signs may seem like what you experienced in your past but give it time, watch, pray and observe carefully so you don't blow any opportunity out of proportion.

Take time to learn from your mistakes. Consider the red flags you ignored, your contribution to those mistakes, your quick judgment and other factors that led to the disappointments and hurts. Something good can come out from learning from such mistakes because at least, they equip you with adequate experience to carry on in life.

Firstly, begin to love yourself, some people go

through abusive relationships over and over again and become so used to being abused so they define themselves with it. Love does not torture, love does not hurt, and it comes freely and willingly.

Luke 9:62 (NIV)

Jesus replied, "No one who puts a hand to the plow and looks back is fit for service in the kingdom of God."

This means if you are done with your past, you don't go digging them out and repeating the same things expecting a different result.

The past is gone, ask God to help you to forget about the way you were cheated on, beaten, hurt, belittled, and disappointed and focus on the new relationship. Enjoy it with every being in you, give genuine love and receive it back, flow with the moment because this is the new "you" to enjoy. It may seem unreal and too good to be true because of what you have been through. But it may end up being like your past if you bring your past hurts into the relationship and if you don't rely on the Holy Spirit to work on your new beginning. Do not punish someone for someone else's sin against you.

Everybody is different, every relationship is different and every scenario is different. Don't look back when you put your hand to the plow. See an opportunity in a new relationship as a new learning process and a new beginning. Give and receive the best from it.

Philippians 3:12 (NIV)

Not that I have already obtained all this, or have already arrived at my goal, but I press on to take hold of that for which Christ Jesus took hold of me.

Press on to achieve a goal, keep pressing on to be victorious, press on no matter the struggles, the stumbling blocks, and the anxieties. If you find new love, press on and work on it to thrive, use the mistakes and learning experiences from the previous relationship as stepping stones to put your current relationship on a pedestal.

John 8:36 (NIV)

So if the Son sets you free, you will be free indeed.

It doesn't matter your faults or failures, the Bible says, you're free indeed. No man can hold your failures and brokenness against you unless you let them, therefore don't drag your past along.

Work on Your Past and Don't Drag it Along

2 Corinthians 5:17 (NIV)
Therefore, if anyone is in Christ, the new creation has come: The old has gone, the new is here!

Healing from your past will enable you to accept love and recognize it but if you do not heal from it, you will not be able to identify true love when you find one and you will not be able to receive and enjoy love. This may in the long run cause you to end up with another wrong or abusive person because your attitude may push the right person away. Leave your past in the past and don't drag it along with you.

CHAPTER 7

Avoid Pretence and Be Yourself

Luke 8:17 (NIV)
For there is nothing hidden that will not be disclosed, and nothing concealed that will not be known or brought out into the open.

I believe nothing can be hidden under the sun and it does not matter how long it takes, it will eventually come out. Due to this, pretenders will get fed up over a period of time and will be caught in their own web. Come clean with your true character in any relationship you find yourself in. Pretence and façade do not thrive well as tools to get into or to stay in a relationship until marriage. The pretence or façade will eventually come crumbling down either before or after the marriage, therefore "BE YOURSELF".

Sometimes, in a bid to attract that beautiful lady or fine gentleman, it's easy to assume the role of a person you are not. For some women for instance, in order to be more attractive, they tend to dress provocatively to win the heart of a man. A person can also put up certain behaviors or even succumb to certain actions that they may naturally not accept. Succumbing to such behaviors sets the precedent for certain actions in the relationship or marriage.

If you present yourself in a certain way to your partner, your partner will expect that behavior to continue in the relationship and also in the marriage. When such behaviors end during the marriage, your partner's expectation will be squashed leading to problems and disappointments.

There was an incident that happened a few years ago. Out of disappointment, a man sued his wife after the honeymoon claiming that his wife's flawless makeup and dressing deceived him into marriage. According to him, she was different without make-up and that was deceitful.

2 Timothy 3:13 (NIV)
while evildoers and impostors will go from bad to worse, deceiving and being deceived.

Certain people also go the extra mile to impress their partners in the form of buying very expensive gifts or borrowing material things to impress each other. When a man does this for instance, he set the precedence for the woman to expect such acts in the marriage because she becomes used to such treatment over a period of time. When it ceases after marriage, reality sets in, the fights, and squabbles begin, people become brokenhearted and feel like they were deceived or lured into the marriage.

Present yourself to the other party just as you are for them to decide whether they like it or not. A deceitful act to woo a man or woman into marriage is a big offense that people find difficult to forgive.

Come clean to your partner and let them know your weaknesses and your strengths.

Sometimes, your weakness may certainly be their strength and your strength their weakness thereby complementing each other beautifully. Don't pretend to like a certain behavior, act, or idea when you know deep in your heart that you detest them. Such behaviors do not end in the dating or courtship period. It rather magnifies itself after the marriage.

1 Samuel 16:7 (NIV)

But the LORD said to Samuel, "Do not consider his appearance or his height, for I have rejected him. The LORD does not look at the things people look at. People look at the outward appearance, but the LORD looks at the heart."

I have realized that if a man is ready to settle, they look beyond the make-up, sophistication, deceit, dress-to-kill, façade, etc. Instead, they look for a woman who will respect them, come with ideas to build a home, advise them to become better off and help them save for the future.

When a woman is ready to settle, she looks for commitment, she is ready to be loved by a man who will treat her like a queen and she looks beyond all the money or status when she truly understands love. The fairytale is very different from reality and if you are used to the fairytale and reality sets in, it gives you a rude shock and breeds trouble. Come clean and just as you are to your partner and build your life together genuinely.

Proverbs 31:30-31 (NIV)
30 Charm is deceptive, and beauty is fleeting;
but a woman who fears the LORD is to be praised.
31 Honor her for all that her hands have done,
and let her works bring her praise at the city gate.

CHAPTER 8

Practice Abstinence

Sex is just not a physical act. It has a spiritual aspect that we take for granted. When you sleep with someone there's an exchange of spirits, so sleeping with multiple men or women will result in different spirits being transferred to you.
The spiritual part has an effect on your physical actions, therefore receiving an unclean spirit from a sex act will result in you doing things that you may not usually do. Premarital sex is the only sin that you commit against God and against your own body.

Practice Abstinence

1 Corinthians 6:18 (NIV)
¹⁸ Flee from sexual immorality. All other sins a person commits are outside the body, but whoever sins sexually, sins against their own body.

God will forgive you for the act or sin, but can you forgive yourself? Can you take that act back? If it is your virginity you lost, can you get your innocence back? In modern times, some singles argue that a sexual encounter with their potential spouse to determine whether they are sexually compatible or the size of organs are the right fit etc. is necessary.

If this argument holds, does that mean that one will be sleeping with all their potential suitors just to determine compatibility and fit? What would you be doing to yourself, what image are you portraying, and at what number will you stop? What if someone has a good character but you feel they're not good in bed? Is marriage only about sex to you?

I believe the more people go through this sampling exercise, the more dissatisfied they would be because they will be comparing their current experience with the previous ones.

This dissatisfaction will eventually trace into marriage and affect a beautiful sex life because a spouse's performance may not match previous experiences.

Some people commit adultery out of disappointment that their spouses do not match up to their previous experiences. This may break a home which will have consequential effects on the children.

Kathy is someone who believed in sampling her suitors and was eventually forced into marrying a man who impregnated her. She didn't love him and could have saved herself from such trouble if she had abstained from pre-marital sex.

As Christians, it takes the help of Christ to be able to overcome the pre-marital desire for sex because sometimes, the soul might be willing not to engage in premarital sex but the body is too weak to resist. One must make a conscious effort to be able to discipline themselves to overcome such acts, if not, you will keep falling until you ruin your life.

1 Thessalonians 4:3-5 (NIV)

³ It is God's will that you should be sanctified: that you should avoid sexual immorality; ⁴ that each of you should learn to control your own body in a way that is holy and honorable, [5] not in passionate lust like the pagans, who do not know God;

It doesn't matter if you made a mistake of having premarital sex, God can correct that wrong and restore you if you let him. All you have to do is to ask him to direct you with a purpose of not allowing yourself to be in situations that will make you fall prey into sexual immorality.

Sleeping with a man will not convince him to marry you. Some women believe if they don't give in to a man's sexual demands, they may dump them for another woman. A man who will dump you will do that regardless of the good sex from you. If a man dumps you after showering you with gifts and taking you out on dates, you have not lost anything even though it may hurt. If he had slept with you and dumped you, you would have lost a whole lot because the sexual experience with you is priceless.

Society's view on pre-marital sex may change but it's still a sin before God and against your own self. Why would someone buy a cow when they can get the milk for free? If all you offer them is sex, why would they want to be serious and get married? Every service they need in marriage is being offered on a silver platter so they already feel like a royal without commitments.

Some people try to use sex to fill a void in their lives. Sex cannot fill the void or emptiness in you neither can it heal your hurt, brokenness, and pain. After the sexual act is over, your problems will still remain and you cannot be having sex 24x7 to forget your woes.

It is only Christ who can heal your brokenness. He has the power to fix and mold you, therefore, resort to him and don't give any man or woman that power to keep using and dumping you. You may be enjoying it and would always want to go back, but how do you honestly feel after you get dumped for another person? Mistakes and accidents happen but that doesn't mean you should keep having them.

2 Timothy 2:22 (NIV)

[22] Flee the evil desires of youth and pursue righteousness, faith, love and peace, along with those who call on the Lord out of a pure heart.

Practice Abstinence

When you take sex off the table in a relationship, it makes it easier for you to think objectively and not from the perspective of sensations from a penis or vagina. You are able to make better decisions to improve your life, position yourselves for God's blessings and know each other better. Sex does not make up the biggest aspect of marriage. You will find out that there's more to marriage than sex.

Sex is the last thing on your mind when your plans in life are not proceeding as you want them. The desire to be sexual during the courtship period may be so high because the devil enjoys seeing you fornicate. After marriage, when you can do it the right way, he puts obstacles in the way thereby creating an avenue for conflicts in the marriage.

The need to gratify our sexual desires causes human beings to make wrong choices. This quest for gratification changes our focus of studying our prospective partner to identify red flags or potential pitfalls.

Ephesians 5:3 (NIV)
³ But among you there must not be even a hint of sexual immorality, or of any kind of impurity, or of

greed, because these are improper for God's holy people.

After the wild sex and infatuation are over, the true character of a person and values emerges. If you get into marriage because your partner is good in bed, sex would be your least priority when the red flags you ignored start appearing.

Things can be so bad when you're married to the wrong person to the extent that, seeing their nudity will not even make you think about sex and you will unintentionally become celibate without knowing. It is better for you to be celibate before marriage than to suddenly experience a forced and rapid celibacy after marriage.

Celibacy in a relationship breeds mutual respect and your judgment will not be clouded. I have met people who told me they built their pre-marital relationship on sex. This hindered their ability to build deep friendship through taking time to study and understand each other. After the marriage, they saw certain behaviors that make them regret saying "I do". Sex clouded their judgments so now they have to endure their marriage.

I always ask myself so many questions when I hear about someone getting pregnant just after a few months of dating their partner. I wonder why no protection was used even if the risk of pre-marital sex was being taken. What if one partner has an STD (Sexually Transmitted Diseases)? The existence of pregnancy indicates that sex was unprotected. Who would have taken the blame if an STD had been contracted? There would surely be bitterness and hatred. This is because, the love they had for each other was not nurtured into maturity, therefore too feeble to withstand such a crisis. Do people take the time to analyze the realities of their decisions?

I remember watching a video where a young lady ended up having sex after her first date with a rich handsome guy. They had very passionate sex in his luxurious apartment even though the gentleman refused to use protection. After she got home that night, she tried to contact him to no avail. A few months later, she went to the hospital because of malaise. Upon several tests by her doctor, it was confirmed that she was pregnant and HIV positive. All her life's dreams and aspirations suddenly flew

Practice Abstinence

away. Just one bad decision to sleep with someone who she thought was Mr. Right snuffled life out of her.

Mistakes happen, but in most cases, people allow their flesh to dictate to them resulting in deep regrets. Pause, think about the what-ifs, and ask yourself what's next after those few minutes of pleasure. Ask yourself if you will be hurt in case you're dumped the next day or how you will feel if the person doesn't even pick up your calls.

Don't allow any man to threaten to leave you if you don't offer sex. You are not an item. Don't allow any woman to call you "dull or a wimp" because you want to be celibate. Your virility will testify of itself when you get married.

1 Corinthians 6:19 (NIV)

[19] Do you not know that your bodies are temples of the Holy Spirit, who is in you, whom you have received from God? You are not your own;

Finally, say "NO" to sex, invest that time into building friendship, getting to know each other's do's and don'ts and focus on your future plans by seeking

God's directions to guide and lead you on the upcoming journey.

Romans 12:1-2 (NIV)

A Living Sacrifice

Therefore, I urge you, brothers and sisters, in view of God's mercy, to offer your bodies as a living sacrifice, holy and pleasing to God—this is your true and proper worship. [2] Do not conform to the pattern of this world, but be transformed by the renewing of your mind. Then you will be able to test and approve what God's will is—his good, pleasing and perfect will.

CHAPTER 9

Sexual Abstinence Doesn't Equate to Ignorance

Knowing and learning the anatomy of both sexes is part of the preparation process for a fun, healthier, pleasurable and a lasting sex life in marriage. In the part of the world where I grew up, talking about sex was considered a taboo and was hardly mentioned or discussed.

The mention of the word "sex" by anyone in public is seen as immoral. People therefore avoid this topic, keeping their imaginations and questions to themselves. This led to some getting misled by the experienced people who prey on their innocence. These days, people are obsessed with sex and it is cheapened with misinformation especially with the advancement of technology. These misinformed and confused young ones end up making mistakes that could have been corrected.

Hosea 4:6 (NIV)

my people are destroyed from lack of knowledge.

"Because you have rejected knowledge,

I also reject you as my priests;

because you have ignored the law of your God,

I also will ignore your children.

With a lack of information on sex, a naïve couple may experience petty problems in the marriage. This may also be in marriages in which one partner is more experienced and does not have the patience to educate the other. Due to the taboo symbol on sex, couples who are having problems relating to that, hesitate to reveal it. They may end up beating around the bush and channeling all their frustrations into petty squabbles.

Sex in marriage was ordained by God and it's not meant for just a particular kind of people but rather for every married couple.

Daniel 1:17 (NIV)

***17** To these four young men God gave knowledge and understanding of all kinds of literature and learning. And Daniel could understand visions and dreams of all kinds.*

Every married couple does it and pretence does not help in any way because whatever happens in each couple's bedroom is known to them alone. When a couple is preparing for marriage, I believe they should invest their time and resources in buying books on sexual education, reading articles and materials on the web, discussing their thoughts with their marriage counselors and mentor.

Answers to bothering question must be sought because just as food is good for the body, so is sex good for the marriage. Some people are misinformed about sex so they see it as gross or nasty. Once you're married, unless one party is not comfortable with a sexual position or act, anything that happens between a man and woman on their matrimonial bed or anywhere between them is honorable before God.

Educating oneself about sex for the future does not entail indulging in watching pornography and resorting to 3rd party sexual substitutes. Pornography is a sin before God and it is the number one killer of natural sexual desire and pleasure in marriage. Some people get so hooked on pornography to the extent that they cannot make love to their spouses. They watch it on their phones, their computers, and every least spare time.

Addiction to pornography starts with the intention of obtaining knowledge but with time, the stage acts become the standard for a gratifying sexual experience. The female actors feign excessive pleasure and the male actors depict abnormal virility (holding an erection for a long time). With these images in mind and the inability to match up to what you see, will result in dissatisfaction and frustration either with oneself or spouse. What is depicted by the actors is possible because they are paid to deliver and medications are taken to enable them to maintain such performances.

The question then is, how long can you get

hooked on an act performed by someone who is paid to make all those noises and stay erect for hours. People who indulge in watching porn often complain of not being sexually attracted to their spouses or they lose the urge for their spouses.

Pornography and its pretences take a hold on them and they eventually deviate from the marriage by going out to seek what they have seen. Knowledge of sex has to be sought for a better sex life in marriage but the right knowledge must be sought from the right places to make the marriage and sex enjoyable.

Proverbs 14:15-18 (NIV)
15 The simple believe anything,
but the prudent give thought to their steps.
16 The wise fear the LORD and shun evil,
but a fool is hotheaded and yet feels secure.
17 A quick-tempered person does foolish things,
and the one who devises evil schemes is hated.
18 The simple inherit folly,
but the prudent are crowned with knowledge.

CHAPTER 10

Don't Jump Into Marriage

We often hear the saying. "All my friends are married or are getting married". It's better late than wrong and so is it better to go into a happy lasting marriage at an older age than go into an early terrible marriage.

One of the most common mistakes people make these days is jumping into marriage prematurely before realizing they were not ready for it.

Candace felt time wasn't on her side and all her friends were getting married, so she was ready to settle for the next available man. A man who knew she was desperate came around and pretended to be in love with her.

She fell head over heels in love and they immediately got married. She got to know the real character of her husband after a few months of marriage. This comprised of unending lies, abuse, womanizing, laziness and insecurity. Her days were filled with tears and regrets until the marriage ended. Her friends had seen all the signs of her husband's repulsive character prior to marriage but she refused to take heed of their warnings just because she wanted a ring to show off.

If Candace had taken her time to study this man, she would have seen the glaring signs of his bad character and would have made a better decision of not jumping into marriage. It is always better to be late than wrong when it comes to marriage.

Singles must make time to assess themselves and their partner's before making a decision that can make or mar them for the rest of their lives. The person you choose to court and marry impacts your life. Marriage does not only involve sex like most people think but rather, both parties have to blend their strengths and weaknesses to complement each other. Don't jump into marriage because you see a rosy marriage around you. Some marriages may seem beautiful outside but may need a lot of work and prayer indoors. Some couples have come a long way at fixing each other, going through various tests etc. which most marriages wouldn't have survived but they picked up the pieces and rebuilt it.

Seeing such rosy-looking marriages without knowing about the background or looking forward to the work that goes into it can be appealing. When a marriage is jumped into, it can easily come with regrets when reality sets in and you're not ready for.

Acts 1:7 (NIV)

He said to them: "It is not for you to know the times or dates the Father has set by his own authority. Waiting for the right man or woman is usually not easy especially as you grow older and age is not on your side. Sometimes, it's hard to keep waiting and believing God to send you the right partner at the right time. But just as the bible stated in Acts 1:7, we cannot know the times or dates certain things will happen in our lives.

Waiting may be for a long period but when the day comes, he certainly makes all things beautiful in order for you to be able to forget the years of waiting. God's time is the right time and he's never late according to his clock. Some people diligently wait for a long time and just when their Boaz or Ruth is around the corner, they miss it by taking a hasty decision that they regret for the rest of their lives.

Wait upon the Lord and while you are at it, socialize, get to know people, look out for red flags, and make the right decision. Get out of your comfort zone and do things for people, work hard on your character if you think it's not a pleasant one, and while at it, develop a positive and great attitude.

Habakkuk 2:3 (NIV)
³ For the revelation awaits an appointed time;
it speaks of the end and will not prove false.
Though it linger, wait for it; it will certainly come
and will not delay.

Sometimes, we will question God, blame ourselves, shed tears, become angry and give up because Mr. Right or Ms. Right is not here. God's timing I believe is never late. WAIT!! So that in hindsight, you will give thanks and be happy that you waited.

Rushing before God's timing will cause you to be in marriage bondage. While waiting, watch, pray, and believe that God is preparing a perfect fit for a spouse for you. If you have such a focus, there will be no anxiety because of a delay in marriage nor will you rush into marrying anybody that comes your way.

Ruth 3:3 (NIV)

³ Wash, put on perfume, and get dressed in your best clothes. Then go down to the threshing floor, but don't let him know you are there until he has finished eating and drinking.

The period of waiting on God to bring your Boaz or your Ruth doesn't mean you give up in life looking shabbily, staying in your home always expecting a man or woman to fall off from the roof," boom" or knock on your door.

Sometimes, due to family pressure, people are forced to marry someone they had a child with. This is in the bid to correct having a child out of wedlock or to protect a family's image. Such marriages sometimes don't work out because the goal of the relationship may not be about marriage from the onset. The process of getting to know each other and deciding whether to take the relationship to the next level may not have materialized before the pregnancy happened. This forced commitment to each other may result into hatred than love for each other. Most often, when a lady becomes pregnant in a relationship, love easily tends to develop into hate for some people.

We take our time to research and shop before we buy a car that we may change within five years, why don't we take more time in researching and getting to know our potential life partner's before we make a decision. Desperation shouldn't push you into getting married to someone you genuinely know you don't love. Look up to God, invest some time into dating and courtship, build deep friendship and let God direct your path in making the right decision.

Wait for the right time, "GOD'S TIMING".

Proverbs 3:5-6 (NIV)

Trust in the LORD with all your heart and lean not on your own understanding; in all your ways submit to him, and he will make your paths straight.

CHAPTER 11

Don't Be Desperate

Men are naturally born to be pursuers of women and if he is truly interested in you, he wouldn't need your help in pursuing you. Even though in modern times some women decide to pursue the men, more often than not when this happens, the man does not put a lot of work into the relationship. If a woman is the one doing all the texting, calling to check on him, planning date nights, etc. that is an obvious sign that he is not into you, therefore, maintain your dignity and put a stop to it.

A man who really loves a woman makes her his priority. He will try to impress and woo her by giving her gifts, and words of love. Others would dispute this fact that men are supposed to be doing the pursuing because of modernization. That's why everyone has their own opinion but as the bible clearly stated, "he who finds a wife" which means the man would have to seek.

Men are natural hunters and a man does not mind driving hours just to spend some time with a woman he's in love with. He can't have enough of her so he will always have an excuse to see his woman or have an unending phone call.

Isaiah 40:31 (NIV)

but those who hope in the LORD will renew their strength. They will soar on wings like eagles; they will run and not grow weary, they will walk and not be faint.

Some women by their actions show the men they are desperate for a relationship or marriage. They will do everything to get and keep the man. The question a woman must ask herself at this point is, why would he put a ring on my finger if he is getting all the benefits of marriage?

Why would I be his priority if I'm dishing myself to him at the least provocation or a threat to end the relationship? Nobody pays for a free service. Even if there is a long line, people will still wait for their turn because it's a free service. Valuable things are usually preserved, cherished and an extra effort is made to keep them so they can last.

Lamentations 3:25 (NIV)

The LORD is good to those whose hope is in him,

to the one who seeks him;

Some people also have the mentality of quickly getting married to solve all their problems. Marriage is not the solution to your problems. What would you do if your problems are not solved after marriage? What if you end up in the role of being the problem solver for your spouse? Will you leave your marriage because the problems that you thought would be solved by getting married is still lingering on or you will stay to fight for your marriage? Some people also have the mentality of spiting friends or family by getting married and this can be another problem waiting to explode on its own. You can spite your friends and family for a moment but if your marriage is in shambles, they will have the last laugh.

In desperation, some people keep or hold on to certain relationships even though they genuinely know it will not end up well in the long run. The people they are in a relationship with, destructs them from meeting their Ruth or Boaz. Some ladies and gentlemen have lost better opportunities to be happily married to their Boaz or Ruth because they were hanging out with a time-waster.

It is better to move on to seek a partner that fits your standard than to be in a relationship with someone with a sub-par standard. Rationally, one may think it's better to keep a diseased bird than to seek a healthy one in the bush but the diseased bird may destruct you from finding the healthy bird.

Take a moment and ask yourself if this is truly working and if this is what you genuinely want for yourself. Pray over it, weigh the options, assess personality, and think about where you see yourself in the next few years before making a decision.

Accept the fact that people cannot be changed and therefore there's no guarantee that the relationship will be better in the future.

Psalm 37:34 (NIV)

*Hope in the L*ORD *and keep his way.*

He will exalt you to inherit the land;

when the wicked are destroyed, you will see it.

Don't be too desperate to keep a man or a woman. If someone wants you, nothing can keep them away from being with you and if they don't want you, nothing you do can make them stay. Never chase anyone to love you because true love will definitely find its way to where it belongs.

Habakkuk 2:3 (NIV)

³ For the revelation awaits an appointed time;

it speaks of the end and will not prove false.

Though it linger, wait for it; it will certainly come and will not delay.

CHAPTER 12

Build Friendship

Some people believe that you can get married to a person without building a friendship but that can happen after marriage. Building friendship before marriage is very valuable and cannot be underrated. A relationship that is grounded in deep friendship can easily withstand the storms of life and have a better chance of surviving. A great friendship helps to build trust, stronger commitment and a value is placed on each other's friendship.

Build Friendship

2 Kings 2:2 (NIV)
*Elijah said to Elisha, "Stay here; the L*ORD* has sent me to Bethel." But Elisha said, "As surely as the L*ORD* lives and as you live, I will not leave you." So they went down to Bethel.*

It is very common these days to see people getting married in a few months after meeting without building a friendship. When the focus is placed on physical attractiveness and lustful sexual desires, time is not made to develop a deep friendship. Most of the couple's time is spent planning the wedding day that would last for only a few hours and no time is invested in the marriage that will last longer than the wedding day.

I strongly believe in getting to really know a person. Build friendship where you can comfortably talk about any topic unendingly and be genuinely comfortable around the person devoid of pretence.

Ecclesiastes 4:9-10 (NIV)
[9] Two are better than one, because they have a good return for their labor: [10] If either of them falls down, one can help the other up. But pity anyone who falls and has no one to help them up.

Over the years, this principle has worked not only for my parents' marriage but other matured marriages I know. Get to know each other and do not be too quick to jump to the planning-a-wedding stage. This is because the focus is shifted from getting to know each other and friendship building but rather, to planning a beautiful ceremony. This ceremony will only last a few hours and may be forgotten in a couple of weeks. After the wedding, the couple will realize that there's more to a peaceful marriage than what meets the eye.

If friendship is not part of the foundation prior to marriage, the marriage will find it very difficult to withstand the ups and downs of life. Some women are more interested in having a ring on their finger than building a friendship. They may even ask the men how soon they plan to put a ring on the finger. Some men, on the other hand, have set up marriage deadlines for themselves and therefore are willing to get married to any woman who is available.

Such relationships can be dangerous if both parties are not on the same page in life or working to achieve the same goal in marriage. This is because such couples are barely friends, barely know each other from Adam and their tolerance level when it comes to dealing with pressure.

Job 16:20-21 (NIV)

[20] My intercessor is my friend
as my eyes pour out tears to God;
[21] on behalf of a man he pleads with God
as one pleads for a friend.

A solid friendship is spiritually crucial. When you build a friendship, it is easier to support each other spiritually. Like the above scripture, a friend will intercede on your behalf and so will your partner who holds you dear to their heart intercede on your behalf in good times and in bad times.

Making time to build a friendship before marriage is not a waste of precious time. It comes very handy when misunderstandings come up. The building of friendship starts with finding what you have in common and accepting your differences. Some relationships or marriages are not built on friendship so they eventually look like a boss and subordinates' relationship. When friendship exists, it makes the relationship enjoyable and much fun. Love and personality get you attracted to each other but they're not enough for a marriage to thrive.

A marriage stands firm with Christ as the center, so is spending quality time, forgiveness, appreciation and respect for one another, celebrating each other, being each other's best friend, etc. Make time to build friendship and don't be the next available man or woman to a person who is ready for marriage.

A firm foundation of friendship is the bedrock for a healthy, fulfilling, romantic and steady marriage. Build a firm foundation and allow Christ to take the wheel.

CHAPTER 13

Set Boundaries

It is very good to set boundaries in a relationship prior to marriage and such boundaries will continue to be honored even after marriage. In any relationship, whether friendship or romantic, you teach people what you tolerate and how you want to be treated by the boundaries you set and your response to their actions.

Luke 23:8-9 (NIV)
[8] When Herod saw Jesus, he was greatly pleased, because for a long time he had been wanting to see

him. From what he had heard about him, he hoped to see him perform a sign of some sort. ⁹ He plied him with many questions, but Jesus gave him no answer.

Jesus in the above scripture set boundaries for himself. He refused to answer when he was asked questions in verse 9. That proves he said no to things he wasn't comfortable with.

If you accept disrespect in your relationship as normal, don't expect otherwise because it will be the same or worse after marriage. Usually, people make the mistake of making excuses for their partners' awful behaviors during the courtship period to the astonishment of those around them. They wonder why such behaviors are accepted even though almost everyone deems it unacceptable.

My dear lady or gentleman, if you have to lose someone because you had to set boundaries or correct their behaviors, they were not meant to be in your life anyway. God has his own way of removing people who don't deserve you from your life. Don't push it. This is because someone who loves you will respect you as an adult and will abide by your dos and don'ts therefore, would not cross certain boundaries. If such a person takes that for granted and you accept it, kiss "respect" goodbye in your relationship.

Matthew 16:23 (NIV)

Jesus turned and said to Peter, "Get behind me, Satan! You are a stumbling block to me; you do not have in mind the concerns of God, but merely human concerns."

If your boundaries are not respected by a person or a partner, do as Jesus did. He said, "get behind me, Satan!" He considered Satan's actions as improper and a stumbling block to his life and fulfillment. He did not entertain him as he deemed his behavior unacceptable. He took an action. Such actions may seem drastic but they are worthwhile. Adults must respect each other's boundaries and know where their freedom ends with someone especially if they claim to love the person and are in a relationship with them.

Matthew 19:16-21 (NIV)

[16] *Just then a man came up to Jesus and asked, "Teacher, what good thing must I do to get eternal*

Set Boundaries

life?" **17** "Why do you ask me about what is good?" Jesus replied. "There is only One who is good. If you want to enter life, keep the commandments." **18** "Which ones?" he inquired. Jesus replied, "'You shall not murder, you shall not commit adultery, you shall not steal, you shall not give false testimony, **19** honor your father and mother, and 'love your neighbor as yourself.'" **20** "All these I have kept," the young man said. "What do I still lack?" **21** Jesus answered, "If you want to be perfect, go, sell your possessions and give to the poor, and you will have treasure in heaven. Then come, follow me."

In this scripture, Jesus was blunt with the rich man for him to sell his possessions to be able to follow him. Sometimes setting boundaries may involve your partner getting rid of certain behaviors and things to be able to follow you or be in a relationship with you. Such valuable things or behaviors could be material or immaterial things that hinder the ability to adhere to your boundaries.

It may be difficult and uncomfortable, but if it is true love and they really want to be with you, they will make such sacrifices as the rich man was asked to do. For him to sell his possessions which of course may have been very expensive or worked very hard to acquire, would have been a big issue for him to battle. With a goal to follow Jesus, he went ahead to fulfill Jesus' requirement though he had the option of rejecting it. Sometimes, the boundaries one may have to set is to make it a point to live apart before marriage.

Some people believe in living together for a period before marriage. This is biblically and morally wrong. I have seen people living together for over 5 years and got divorced within 2 years of marriage. One may wonder what happened in those 2 years of marriage that did not happen in the 5 years of cohabitation leading to divorce. People have walked the cohabitation path and have had regrets.

Living together before marriage does more harm than good to a Christian because the bible is against it and people feel used and dumped if it goes down badly. Cohabitation is playing a mock-marriage where commitment is not required therefore, there's no zeal to work on issues that come up in the relationship. Don't live together before marriage.

Set Boundaries

People have their theories to back the notion of how good it is to live together before marriage but most people who search their hearts after some years regret it but may not come out to speak the truth.

Luke 16:13 (NIV)

13 "No one can serve two masters. Either you will hate the one and love the other, or you will be devoted to the one and despise the other. You cannot serve both God and money."

Two masters cannot be served at the same time. You either win one's heart and lose the other or lose both. You cannot affirm Christ's love and agree to your partner's request of living together before marriage when you know it's biblically wrong. Such boundaries must be made clear from the onset of the relationship and must be respected by both parties no matter how hard things are financially.

Some people use financial constraints as an excuse to live together. Had you not met your partner, where would you be living? That period of getting to know each other before marriage is not a decade and sacrifices here and there must be made to protect your dignity.

Set Boundaries

Setting boundaries in a relationship serve as the stepping stones for the relationship to thrive and creates a barrier to prevent arbitrary behaviors. When boundaries are adhered to in a relationship, respect tends to dwell in it and everybody plays their part effectively. With boundaries, each party knows when to say yes or no.

If boundaries are set at the beginning of a relationship, it eliminates chaos. This is because it sets the tone for the relationship, thus, where one's freedom to do something begins and ends is known. It explicitly lays down the foundation for a safe, comfortable and sound relationship.

Don't lower your standards to keep a failing relationship. Set boundaries that must be respected by both of you in order for love, peace, respect, and understanding to reign in the relationship and your marriage. "DON'T LOWER YOUR STANDARDS".

CHAPTER 14

Why Do I Date the Wrong People?

Sometimes, how you present yourself paves the way for dating wrong people. When such a situation keeps happening in your life, it's time to sit down and do some self-evaluation in order to pinpoint what in your spirit, personality, behavior or judgment is contributing to the attraction of the wrong people.

Romans 12:2 (NIV)
Do not conform to the pattern of this world, but be transformed by the renewing of your mind. Then you

will be able to test and approve what God's will is— his good, pleasing and perfect will.

By the renewing of your mind like the bible stated, you transform and change the way you perceive things and people who come your way in the bid to know you and to start a relationship. You will at this point therefore be able to test the motives of your prospective partners and also to decipher their true intentions.

God's will is for you to date and be in a great relationship with the right person for your happiness to be fulfilled. He cares about even the little things in your life and therefore if you involve him in making decisions, he will certainly direct your path.

Are you appearing to the opposite sex as lonely, desperate, not fulfilled, a sex object or having a low self-worth? You have to be really honest with yourself, delve deep into yourself, your past, your parent's relationship, etc. It is very vital to decide on the type of woman or man you want to attract. If you are the type that everything a person says to woo you flies with you, that's the kind of person you will attract. If you are the type who is materialistic and flirty, that is the kind of person you will attract. Which of these are you? Your actions determine if you are ready for the man or woman God has in store for you. Good and caring men still exist and so are virtuous and sweet women.

I remember back in college, I had more male friends than females and these male friends were very open and upfront with me. Most of them told me the kind of women they wanted as wives and the kind they just wanted as girlfriends. I was told that the girlfriend types were the ones who always presented themselves easy to get and who wear skimpy revealing clothes. According to them, the reason why they cannot marry such ladies is that they cannot present them to their mothers since they will be disappointed in them.

I learned a lot from these guys which helped me with the reality of what a man really wants to see in a woman to enable them to confirm she is the one. I further asked, what if the lady you may present has been pretending all this while? Some of them said, "at least I tried", some said, they would end the relationship. They still wanted a sexually attractive woman but not one who portrayed herself as if she was going to dish it out to the whole world.

Some of them would not even want their friends to see them with such ladies during the day so they sneak to spend time with them at night. This broke my heart because such ladies felt they were the hot ones on campus but sadly, these guys thought otherwise though they patronized them.

I felt that was selfish on the part of the men but they also justified their behaviors by saying that it was what the ladies truly wanted with no absolute commitment. This affirms the notion that you attract what you reflect or "who you attract is a reflection of who you are" which may sometimes be wrong.

Jeremiah 29:11 (NIV)

[11] For I know the plans I have for you," declares the LORD, "plans to prosper you and not to harm you, plans to give you hope and a future.

It doesn't matter who the world or friends deem fit for you to date. God's plan for you is never wrong and will come to pass if you wait on him. Your relationship desires are in his plans and with the right attitude and mindset, you will accomplish that joyous goal.

In looking out to date the right kind of people, ask the Holy Spirit to help you to decipher whether it is the right relationship or not. Always take time to get to know a person. Do not rush a relationship. Give time an opportunity and watch the other party in different settings of life. How they react in various situations will also tell you a lot about them. It is worth the time to be patient to see someone's true colors.

To truly know a person, observe the way they treat other people such as family members, friends, colleagues, or even the cashier at the store. The way they treat them will give you an idea of how you will be treated in a relationship. In their bid to impress you, they would obviously show their good side. After habituation sets in, you will see their true behavior.

2 Corinthians 6:17 (NIV)
Therefore, "Come out from them and be separate, says the Lord. Touch no unclean thing, and I will receive you."

The above scripture talks about setting ourselves apart from the masses or the ordinary. Setting yourself apart means putting yourself on a pedestal that is uncommon to the norm. It doesn't mean it may happen overnight by grabbing the perfect gentleman or lady you want.

It may take a little more time, but wait for it. Don't drown in the habit of always meeting and dating the wrong people. Your Mr. Right or Mrs. Right still exists, therefore, make time to find them for a great and peaceful relationship.

CHAPTER 15

Prepare To Be a Godly Wife or Husband

Praying to God to bring you a Godly spouse is a great thing. But the question is, are you prepared to be a godly wife or husband? Are you ready for God to mold you to become a godly spouse worthy and presentable?

Woman: Are you prepared to be a virtuous woman filled with wisdom while possessing a gentle and quiet spirit, walk in forgiveness and being a good communicator? Are you ready to lend Mr. Right a helping hand for him to achieve his life's purpose or destiny? Is it all about you and what you can gain from the relationship? Are you ready to be his support system and greatest cheerleader?

Proverbs 31:30 (NIV)

Charm is deceptive, and beauty is fleeting;

but a woman who fears the LORD is to be praised.

Most men are incomplete without their women cheering them on, looking out for them, and being their third eye. Most men can barely multitask because they focus on one goal at a time and they are task-oriented. This sometimes becomes a problem when you need certain things done for you.

As a Godly wife, will you accept or nag about those weaknesses? His weakness may be your strength and if you specialize in that area for him to depend on your strength, he feels secure with you and looks up to you. If you nag about his shortfalls or weaknesses, he feels threatened and will become defensive. His weaknesses should be communicated to him in a nice and pleasant way for him not to feel attacked and belittled to become defensive.

Men get tired of women who nag at every little problem or make mountains out of molehills. This drains them and according to some men, it prevents them from going home after a long and hectic day at work. Men expect the home to be peaceful and welcoming when they get there, therefore blowing every little problem out of proportion creates drama and tension in the relationship.

It is also advisable to keep friends out of your marriage. This is because no one needs to know your marital business, therefore, keep your problems, decisions, plans etc. in-house. Make it a point not to ever speak negatively about your fiancé' or husband to your friends and family. If you do, that is the lens through which they see him and you tell the world the level of respect that should be accorded to him by the way you portray him.

Your husband is the head of the household, therefore, give him the opportunity to lead while praying to God to lead him on the right path. A man values respect more than sex and if he is respected, he will build his kingdom for you and make you his queen. Respecting your man doesn't make you a weakling or a subordinate, neither does it diminish your power or status. You possess a lot of power as a woman and if you do not know how to use that power to influence decisions in your home, you will resort to nagging, disrespect, and eventually become an angry or a bitter woman.

Most men are attracted to a woman with a good sense of humor who can make them laugh by their witty jokes to help them de-stress therefore develop a sense of humor to make jokes and not to be serious all the time.

A godly woman must also develop a listening ear and patient spirit where her husband can feel very comfortable to tell her his thoughts, desires, fears, etc. without being judged or criticized.

Man: If you're not grounded in the Lord, how can you set an altar for the Lord for your family to follow? You are going to be their leader and a leader who does not know where he is going will always mislead its followers to nowhere.

Joshua 24:15 (NIV)
*[15] But if serving the L*ORD *seems undesirable to you, then choose for yourselves this day whom you will*

*serve, whether the gods your ancestors served beyond the Euphrates, or the gods of the Amorites, in whose land you are living. But as for me and my household, we will serve the L*ORD*."*

Joshua in the above verse spoke about setting the altar for the Lord because he knows he would lead his family to serve the Lord in spirit and in truth. It didn't matter which god others were serving or bowing to. He affirmed that as for him and his family, nothing can stop them from serving the one true God.

As the man of the house, do you see yourself affirming this before men and before God? Do you see yourself practicing it daily for it to permeate every aspect of your life? You have to make that decision if you want Christ to steer the affairs of your household.

Luke 6:38 (NIV)
[38] Give, and it will be given to you. A good measure, pressed down, shaken together and running over, will be poured into your lap. For with the measure you use, it will be measured to you."

A godly man must be willing to give all of himself and share his resources with his wife. Withholding resources from your household is not a quality of a good leader and a servant of God. Christ entreated us to give and it will be given back unto us pressed down, shaken together and running over. Giving should not only be financial but it is giving all that you can offer in service too.

Are you ready to share your financial information and finances? Are you ready for your phone to be an open book that can easily be assessed by your wife? Do you know some women can shop for hours and would want you around them during shopping? Are you ready to watch romantic movies (chick-flicks) with her and be with her in the kitchen cooking for the family?

Be ready to tell your wife and show her how much you appreciate and love her daily and not occasionally. Always place her above everyone else in your life because a woman who truly feels loved, appreciated, and safe with you will always go above and beyond what you can imagine. Don't create an environment where she has to beg for your attention or give her a reason to feel jealous because of your behavior. Be a good listener and provide maximum emotional support because women love to talk and bare their hearts out.

Cooking is a skill that can be learned by both men and women hence try learning such a skill to occasionally surprise her with good food or be in the position to cook when you get home before her. Make her breakfast on weekends when both of you are home, help her clean the home without her asking. Don't leave all the household chores to her, she is not stronger than you are. Help her around the house by cleaning. If you're not good at doing any chore, join her in doing them and you will eventually learn for your home to be peaceful.

Women love such surprises especially when you do nice things for no reason, which could earn you a good treat. Prepare to love your wife like Christ loved the church and discover her love language. Always be honest with her, keep to your words to win her trust because trust takes a long time to be built and a few seconds to be lost.

As a man, lead your family in the right direction and this can only be accomplished by leaning on God for direction. Don't take your wife for granted and don't forget special days such as anniversaries, birthdays, Valentine's Day, mother's day etc. They mean a lot to her. Don't make assumptions because she cannot read your mind.

1 Peter 3:7 (NIV)

Husbands, in the same way be considerate as you live with your wives, and treat them with respect as the weaker partner and as heirs with you of the gracious gift of life, so that nothing will hinder your prayers.

The Bible in the above scripture talks about dealing with your wife with understanding and being considerate with her. Wisdom from above is a much-needed commodity when it comes to dealing with women. They may for instance, wake up and say they're not feeling too good. When you ask them what is wrong, they may say nothing or cannot pinpoint what it is. Though a joke depicts a woman's manual to be 20x bigger than a man, it's a fact.

Colossians 3:19 (NIV)
Husbands, love your wives and do not be harsh with them.

Always make your feelings known to her even when it hurts. Even if you made a mistake, communicate it to her and leave the decision to her rather than hide them from her.

Women have more words than men, therefore, they love to communicate their feelings in words and may sometimes repeat themselves. Are you are a good listener or ready to listen to all her rants and feelings? Sometimes, all she needs is a good listener who will make her feel good by the feedback you give in terms of nodding, sighing with undivided attention. Some men will claim to be listening but their concentration may be on something else and this brings trouble and a gap in communication. She would always want to know if she can speak to you even about the petty troubles that bother her. She would like to tell you things she cannot tell her family or friends.

Are you ready to be trustworthy, will you be her confidant and will not betray her with information she shares with you? Don't stop dating her in marriage. She will still be looking forward to the nice treats, date nights, wooing and pampering just like your courtship phase. Sing nice love songs to her to describe her personality and to tell her how much you appreciate her. Don't guard your phone like your life depends on it, because it causes a lot of tension, suspicion, and mistrust.

Don't love a woman because of her shape, curves, slenderness, beauty, etc. what if all those features diminish after marriage or after your first child. Would you leave her because of that? Will you be frustrated because she's changed?

Romans 12:1 (NIV)

A Living Sacrifice

Therefore, I urge you, brothers and sisters, in view of God's mercy, to offer your bodies as a living sacrifice, holy and pleasing to God—this is your true and proper worship.

A Godly man finds satisfaction in his own wife. Are you prepared to be sexually fulfilled only by your wife and forget all the other women you find pretty and attractive? It is a decision you eventually have to make. Your wife is the only person prepared and approved by God to satisfy you sexually. It doesn't matter what you see out there that looks more attractive than your wife. If it is appealing, attractive and mouth-watering than you think your wife is, exercise self-control because you would always see someone prettier and more attractive. If you behold your wife to be highly attractive and prettier in your sight and mind, you would not make time for any woman who presents themselves to you.

Will you be able to stand firm and grounded when the temptation of adultery knocks on your door? God knows your heart and knows your answer to this question. Flee from such temptations. Don't water it down or lead it on and don't assume hanging around will solve the problem. The Bible says *FLEE*.

1 Corinthians 6:18 (NIV)
Flee from sexual immorality. All other sins a person commits are outside the body, but whoever sins sexually, sins against their own body.

Being married requires you to be selfless. If you're not ready to share things with your spouse, you are not ready to say "I do". If you don't understand your role as a husband or wife in a marriage, it affects the family and society as a whole. In preparation for marriage, you should be able to do these things or achieve them.

Above all, picture your daughter or son being married to someone like you and if that makes you smile, feel good about yourself but if that makes your heart skip a beat, work on yourself. Don't do things to your spouse that you wouldn't want any man or woman to do to your son or daughter. Love her as you love and cherish your own body.

CHAPTER 16

Will I be Sexually Compatible?

Sexual compatibility is a major topic some singles usually ask and are worried about. There are so many unanswered questions regarding this issue. Indulging in premarital sex doesn't guarantee that you and your spouse will be sexually compatible during the marriage. Many have had their sex life dwindle after the honeymoon period though they engaged in premarital sex. This is because the requirements and pressures of daily living may have an effect on the marriage and therefore, couples would have to learn to adjust to ensure intimacy and a vibrant sex life.

Sexual compatibility in marriage happens over a period of time. Compatibility involves adjusting to meet the demands of daily pressures while making sex and intimacy a priority. After a period of time, couples also learn and get to know each other's erogenous zones, how they like the act, etc. With effective communication and correction, couples become experts of their spouse's sexual needs thereby making them sexually compatible.

Most men frankly tell me that they feel they are not sexually compatible with their wives because of differences in sexual urges. Typically, men have higher sexual urges than women. The solution to such a problem is to work out a compromise.

There is no measuring tool to check sexual compatibility between a man and a woman before and after marriage. Sleeping with multiple partners in the bid to find a sexually compatible partner is just a waste of time and it's irrational. What will you do if you think someone is sexually compatible with you but has a bad character?

CHAPTER 17

Communication is a Vital Tool

Listen to understand what is being said, don't listen to give a response. Communication is a key to a great relationship. Communication is a two-way street which must be clearly understood by both parties and feedback must be given to confirm understanding. The journey before and after marriage is smoother when communication is taken very serious by both parties. There is nothing like too much communication in a marriage. Dissemination of information in marriage is a vital tool to keep the marriage going since nobody is a mind reader and one is accountable to their partner for every word that comes from their mouth.

Matthew 12:37 (NIV)
For by your words you will be acquitted, and by your words you will be condemned."

With this in mind, information pertaining to every aspect of your life is disseminated especially when the relationship is going further into marriage. Any information you think your prospective spouse should know must come directly from you for future sake. If you wait for a third party to reveal such information, they will do it the way they deem fit.

They may add or subtract vital information, they may guess and exaggerate, the timing may be wrong, the words may not come out well and it may serve as a betrayal to end your courtship or marriage. You can never underestimate the power of rumor-mongers and haters who can dig into your past to expose and magnify any tiny skeleton in your closet. They will do this just to embarrass you or cause you to be in trouble with your partner. No matter how egregious the information may be, find an appropriate way and time to divulge such information so that your spouse can decide on what to do regarding such information. Taking such a step may protect you in the future because no one can use it against you knowing that your partner is already aware of it. One may ask, what if I tell them and they end the relationship? That is another factor to deal with but the question is, how long can you hold on to such information while it hangs heavily on your conscience.

It can easily prevent you from enjoying your marriage. Pray about it, ask the Holy Spirit to direct you on what to say and how to say it. This is usually because our past always comes back to haunt us and there should be no surprises for our partners when the past decides to creep in.

If communication is effective in the relationship, it opens the door for trust and kicks pretence away from it. With communication, you get to know how many children you may want to have in the future, what place friends and family members can have in the marriage, how to deal with in-laws, finances, children, etc.

Communication is a Vital Tool

Proverbs 18:13 (NIV)
To answer before listening—that is folly and shame.

Effective communication is when you listen to your partner and give feedback. A good listener makes it easy for a person to open up and trust them with information. If communication is devoid of lies, assumptions, pretence, and errors, it creates a unifying bond between you two which helps in building trust in the relationship. Trust takes a while to build up and if it is broken, it takes time to be rebuilt, therefore, don't take it for granted if you truly want a peaceful and loving relationship. Avail yourself to be trustworthy to your spouse at all times and be truthful with your dealings with them.

Communication is considered the lifeblood of a fulfilling relationship. It must be taken seriously and efforts must be made to build upon it daily. Avoid distortion by eliminating jargons or words that the other party may not understand. It must be detailed, clear and straightforward, devoid of distractions, assumptions, and suspicion. Once you leave room for suspense, trust is lost and communication becomes meaningless.

CHAPTER 18

Do You Think You're Ready to Say "I do"?

Discuss each other's expectations about marriage. After all is said and done through the months or years of courtship, do you find peace within yourself to affirm readiness for marriage? Have you assessed yourself from the beginning of the relationship till present to confidently say with beaming smiles that you are ready to say "I do"? I believe this is the time to ask yourself questions and discuss what you expect in marriage. Find ways to work on outstanding issues which involves a heart-to-heart talk.

In marriage, couples don't argue to win or keep score of who said the most words. Some people pride themselves in winning arguments with friends and they take that into the marriage. I sometimes hear some people tell their friends that they have never lost an argument with their spouses. If you aim at winning an argument, you're not being truthful to yourself or your spouse.

This is because you try to ignore the facts and focus on points that would make you win instead of solving the problem at stake. If you are ready for marriage, you must purpose in your heart that arguments should barely be a part of it. Even if they arise, you have to deal with issues maturely, fairly and be sure every party put their genuine points across.

Defense mechanism doesn't work in a marriage where you're always defensive over little stuff even before the other party says a word. If you're wrong, accept it and don't apportion blame. Instead of flipping the blame onto the other party, ask what you did wrong and how it can be fixed. Measures should also be taken for such a situation not to repeat itself.

What may not be a big deal to you may be a big deal to the other party. We were created differently, therefore, accept the differences and treat hurts, pains or situations accordingly. If your partner tells you they were hurt, don't trivialize it but rather talk politely about it and apologize for peace to prevail.

Do you know there are behaviors that affect and kill marriages over a period? Some of these killer-behaviors may be trust issues, when couples decide to keep secrets, when you harbor unforgiveness, lack of communication, lack of respect, infidelity, lies, uncontrolled anger, battering, etc.

Are you ready to support your spouse to upgrade themselves academically, socially and spiritually? I have come across certain people who complain about their spouses attaining higher positions and laurels in society.

Some men, for example, feel threatened when their wives decide to further their education or venture to hold higher positions in society. Some go to the extent of belittling their women with the "you can't do it" words and attitude. They go the extra mile to frustrate such women by stressing them with chores, children and marital issues for them not to have time and ability to embark on higher ventures.

Some also cannot stand the idea of their wives earning more than they do and therefore blow every misunderstanding or correction by their wives out of proportion. This is because they feel their wives attitude is as a result of them earning more than them. It is not stated anywhere in the bible that men should earn higher than women or be more educated than them.

Some women also aim at not supporting their husbands to attain higher academic laurels and positions because they believe the higher they go, the less time they would have for them or they may indulge in extra-marital affairs. In marriage, building each other up to realize their full potential is a vital tool because it makes you part of their success story.

No matter the position or status your spouse attains, they come back to you as their husband or wife. Their position or academia shouldn't take away the role of a husband or wife. The role of a husband or wife does not involve social names or positions given in the office, for example, Boss, Manager, Professor, Pastor, etc.

These positions and titles must be left in the office or place of work for colleagues, peers, and subordinates and be who you are at home. The President's wife doesn't address him as President at home nor all other titles. Confusing roles, positions, and titles with the roles at home bring chaos and misunderstanding.

If you're ready to say "I DO", you have to factor these things into your lifestyle. You have to create room for your spouse to grow and live to their fullest potential without you feeling threatened, but rather accepting it as part of the marriage and be happy with it.

Insecurity is a slow poison of a relationship. It kills it gradually by eating into your thoughts and actions. If you're not endowed with the ability to go higher in education or at your job, don't pull your partner down with you.

Encourage them, find ways to make life easier and allow them to go as high as they can. You may also have strength in areas which your partner is weak in and that means you're vital too. Support in prayer and give your all for your partner to excel for a joint victory.

If you're not ready to accommodate or sacrifice into achieving all of the above, you definitely need more time to prepare for marriage. If you're selfish and believe in using the "I" instead of using "We" or "Us", you are not ready for a happy, fulfilling and peaceful marriage.

CHAPTER 19

The Wedding Day is Less Than 10 hours, Plan it Wisely

Plan the wedding the way you want it and let people know where you stand in terms of budgeting, etc. Let them fall in line because the day is about the two of you, don't break your bank nor invest your retirement funds into it. Neither should you apply for a huge credit or loan because of a program that will last less than 10hrs. The lovely and extravagant wedding to show off does not help the marriage in any way because, after the beautiful ceremony, you may have a buyer's remorse by asking, "was this worth the money invested"? How am I going to settle the outstanding bills? Did I really use all my savings on the wedding?

Proverbs 2:6-8 (NIV)

⁶ For the LORD gives wisdom; from his mouth come knowledge and understanding. ⁷ He holds success in store for the upright, he is a shield to those whose walk is blameless, ⁸ for he guards the course of the just and protects the way of his faithful ones.

The ceremony and its details will be forgotten by the guest of your wedding within a few weeks, therefore, be more concerned about the details that go into the marriage. The detail of the marriage equips you to stand and not to run away at the sight of the least trouble and pressure.

Some women usually want to have a dream fairytale wedding and don't even think about life after the wedding. A fairytale wedding is very nice and appealing to the eye but it doesn't warrant breaking the bank and starting a marriage with huge debts. If you are financially sound and that fairytale wedding will be a drop in the bucket financially, that is perfectly fine but if it is the opposite, it is not worth it. Some people fall in so much debt after the wedding and they end up falling on friends for grocery and payments of bills. Don't overstretch your budget to impress family and friends or to spite your single friends.

Proverbs 18:15 (NIV)
The heart of the discerning acquires knowledge,
for the ears of the wise seek it out.

You may spite or impress them for few hours but the debt is on you and that can start trouble in your beautiful marriage because you have to squeeze to meet your financial obligations or keep working for longer hours.

The friends and families you impressed will be sleeping in the comfort of their bed while you work to pay for the most expensive 10hours of your life. During the planning period, it is time to ask yourselves questions such as, "is it worth borrowing money for a ceremony that would last for a few hours? Are we financially independent to be able to afford an extravagant wedding with no regrets? If we spend our entire savings on a ceremony, how comfortably would we begin our lives together? A beautiful, elegant and memorable wedding ceremony is lovely and worth talking about but should it break the bank? Do the ceremony your own way and style. Give your best shot, look great, feel good about yourselves, make it memorable, be happy but apply wisdom by considering your unique situation. It is just for a few hours but the marriage is a long journey. Use wisdom in all thy dealings.

Proverbs 3:13-18 (NIV)

[13] Blessed are those who find wisdom, those who gain understanding, [14] for she is more profitable than silver and yields better returns than gold.

[15] She is more precious than rubies; nothing you desire can compare with her. [16] Long life is in her right hand; in her left hand are riches and honor.

[17] Her ways are pleasant ways, and all her paths are peace.

[18] She is a tree of life to those who take hold of her; those who hold her fast will be blessed.

CHAPTER 20

During and After the Honeymoon

Ideally, the honeymoon period is the period when both parties tend to know each other sexually and explore each other's bodies to their satisfaction and happiness. During this period, a couple secludes themselves and either go away on a vacation, sightseeing or stay in their home devoid of visits from friends and family. This period is the "aha" moment when it dawns on you that you're truly married and beginning a life together.

During and After the Honeymoon

This period is usually one of the sweetest stages of the marriage where everything seems new to you especially if you waited and was celibate during the relationship. A virgin lady at this period will usually be shy and wonder how her first experience is going to feel like and whether it will hurt, be sweet, sour or sweet and sour. A virgin male will also be wondering how well he may need to perform and whether it would be impressive. All these thoughts will run through your mind and become a distraction which may affect your performance.

A couple should relax and go with the flow. This is where knowledge about things you've heard, researched or been counseled on would come into play. Just be yourself and enjoy intimacy and even if it doesn't go as expected, there are more days, months and years to keep trying to be an expert at it according to your taste and desires.

Take time to teach each other your likes and dislikes or what you're uncomfortable with when it comes to sex. Since both of you are independent adults who know what you want and what you don't, try to respect each other's wishes and opinion.

During and After the Honeymoon

After the weeks or months after the honeymoon period, real life begins for the two of you. This is when you may see certain behaviors and actions you may have never seen during the dating and courtship period or you may have seen them but downplayed them thinking they may change. Viola!! This period may come as a shocker to you especially if you rushed into getting married without getting to know each other to prepare you enough for certain behaviors.

What would you do if you realize that after 6 months or a year, that sweet man or woman you loved and married had changed or is exhibiting his or her true character? Would you leave, try to fix it, be depressed, be disappointed, tell the whole world, or coil in your shell? Would you develop a bad attitude towards the person, refuse to come home early to avoid the person, seek solace in friends, family, another man or woman, etc.?

These are some of the things you have to think about prior to fixing the wedding date and be sure you have an answer to all the above questions before deciding.

Some behaviors may come to you as a surprise in the early years of marriage which is normal because you cannot know a person thoroughly since you can't read minds. Some of the surprising behaviors that you may see, had red flags or signals that you probably may have ignored because all you wanted was to get married.

The opportunity to curb or put a stop to it prior to marriage is lost, therefore, cease the opportunity now to help make a change and ask Christ to help you.

Put an effort into your marriage just like you do with your job. Don't leave the marriage at the least provocation, conflict or pressure. It may take some time but prayer, change in behavior and effort will make it work by the grace of God. If you respect, love and cherish each other, marriage will not be too much work for you. Enjoy your union with Christ's love.

Questions to Ponder On

Do I feel I'm going to be in bondage?

What's my understanding of marriage?

Do I feel I'm being controlled?

Can I be there for my partner when are odds are against them?

Am I ready to be an open book for my partner to know everything about me?

Am I getting married because of material things that can fade away?

Do I like the way we settle our differences?

Am I withholding any information from him/her?

Have we been through Marriage Counseling?

Am I willing to be patient and compromise in situations?

Am I ignoring red-flags?

What are my expectations for marriage?

Is this what I really want or I just want to be married?

What am I bringing to the table to make the marriage complete?

Am I ready to spend the rest of my life with this person?

How do I deal with my in-laws?

Are you prepared to become a wife or a husband?

NOTES

Final Thought

Just like you put much work into your career, hobbies, and others, so should you put more work in a relationship or a marriage for it to be a success story. Endeavor to build a deep friendship before you make a decision to get married. Develop a great sense of humor, learn to communicate effectively, make Christ the center of your union and remember, apologizing and forgiveness doesn't make you a weakling but makes you human. When complacency creeps into a marriage, the fire in it creeps out resulting in a downward spiral.

We fight to keep our properties and things we have worked for. Be committed to fighting for your marriage when you say "I do". Don't walk out from it at the least provocation, fault or disappointment. Cherish and guard it with your heart. Singleness, dating and courtship period ceases the moment you say "I do" which begins a covenant agreement. It is a package that comes with its ups and downs, good days and bad days, therefore seek the counsel of the Holy Spirit to lead you on this journey. Seek good marriage counseling tips that you will always refer to in the marriage and you will never regret it. Marriage is what you make of it and the measure you put in it is what becomes of it.

Dropping the "I" to behold the "We or Us" makes a marriage successful. It is a union that must be enjoyed and not endured. Remember, true love will never come back to you void. Choose wisely, give it your all, keep on loving one another and always remember that many waters cannot quench love and rivers cannot drown it.

Thank you.

Acknowledgments

I thank God for his faithfulness, for preserving my life and for giving me the ability to write my second book. May His name be praised. Amen.

Kofi my love, I will continue to bless God always for your life. What can I say other than to extend my gratitude to you for always believing in me, being my confidant, constantly going through my manuscript to help make an impact. Thank you for your immense support and for demonstrating agape love to me. Without your encouragement, proofreading, and being the third eye, this book wouldn't have come this far. I doff my hat to you.

To my Lovely children; Nuna, Nyanyui, and Neyram, you're my greatest cheerleaders; I love you with all my heart and absolutely love being your mom.

To my Dad, Cephas, thank you for all the sacrifices you made to make me who I am today. Thank you for building my self-esteem and for always believing Selasi "can do" it.

To my dear (Late) Mom, Charity, thank you for teaching me to set boundaries and to believe in myself. Thank you for instilling great values and principles in me. It has made me a great lady and I'm passing it on. Thank you.

About the Author

Selasi graduated with a Bachelor of Science, in Psychology and Political Science (double major) from the University of Ghana and has an Advanced Certificate in Marketing from the Chartered Institute of Marketing,(CIM) United Kingdom (UK). She also graduated from the University of Maryland University College with a Master of Science in Project Management.

She is an Author, an Avid researcher and a Marriage Counselor who enjoys motivating others and her hobbies are events planning, singing, and helping people. She is very detailed-oriented, principled, objective and diligent.

Selasi gives everybody she meets an opportunity and likes to make an impact on people's lives. She loves to speak up for the helpless, fights against injustice and loves to pen her thoughts to inspire and motivate people. Selasi believes in giving genuine love to people because if love is not genuine, it isn't love in the first place.

She is the author of "Let Your Marriage Shine" (Ingredients to Boost Your Marriage).

Made in the USA
Middletown, DE
06 December 2018